Selfishness and Self-Deception: How to Stop It from Ruining Your Relationships

By Ted Dawson

Table of Contents

Introduction

Hello, and welcome to this short eBook on Selfishness and Self-Absorption: How to Stop It from Ruining Your Relationships. Every relationship is as different as the people who make it up. Relationships are deep, complex, beautiful and ineffable, and each is completely unique. All this is true, and we all know it. And yet, it seems like we all tend to fall into the same pitfalls. Why is that? Why is it so hard to overcome selfishness?

Much of the time, we make the same mistakes we've seen our parents make. We emulate, consciously or unconsciously, the behavior we've seen in others. Consequently, many of us have had the experience of finding our cherished relationships fall apart, or become difficult and sour.

While the study of love and relationships could fill entire libraries, in this short book we will talk about one of the most prevalent relationship problems encountered by people of all walks of life. From all social and economic backgrounds, across gender lines and cultural and religious groups, whether young or old, the most common obstacle to realizing the wonderful potential of our relationships comes from **selfishness** and **self-absorption**, which are after all two terms for the same thing, the out of control ego.

But what does it mean to be self-absorbed? How and why does it happen? And why is it so common? More importantly, how can you improve yourself and overcome a character trait that is so common and seems so human? These are the topics we will address in the following short chapters

Chapter 1: Selfishness and Unconditional Love

What is Selfishness?

The first important thing to recognize is that selfishness is a human characteristic, and it belongs to all of us. None of us is selfish all of the time, but each of us is selfish sometimes. This book is all about learning to monitor yourself, so that you become more conscious and aware of your own selfish behavior, and learn to recognize when it is inappropriate. Harmony in life is like harmony in music; it's all about balance.

Simply put, there are two parts that make up selfishness, and these parts always go together. The first part is mental. Selfishness is a way of thinking, a mental perspective and approach to problem solving in which the interests of the person doing the thinking are given the most value.

In life, we are always being presented with choices, which means we are always comparing and evaluating alternatives. Whenever you're evaluating two or more possible courses of action and you think "which of these choices would be better *for me*?," you are engaging in selfish thinking. Of course, we're making decisions constantly, and we do it so quickly that we don't often recognize the thought process we are using. But if you're decisions are being made based on the criteria of what *you want* at any given time, well, that's selfishness.

Of course, selfishness isn't just about how we think. It's also about what we *do*. And that's the second part of selfishness, selfish behavior. Often in life, we act and react so quickly or instinctively to things that are going on around or happening to us that we don't consciously *think* about what we are doing. We aren't acting as much as *reacting*. While we tend to imagine ourselves as being highly intellectual, rational beings, the truth is that so much of our behavior is based on learned patterns. Usually, we have very little awareness of these patterns, as they constitute our unconscious mind. A simple example of this is in the manners we all learn from a young age. We say "please" and "thank you" probably dozens of times a day, but how much thought do we put into doing it?

If you want to perform an experiment, try going just a single day without saying please or thank you. You might find it's not so hard to do with your friends and family. But with strangers, it's often really difficult *not* to use the manners we've been conditioned to use since we were children.

Of course, being polite isn't really a problem, even if we aren't aware of ourselves as we do it. Maybe manners are a nice thing. But unfortunately, there are all kinds of subtler, more deeply ingrained patterns of behavior which we are even less aware of, and some of these can be quite negative.

Selfishness is one of these. While it is true that humans are social animals, it's also true that, for all sorts of biological, social and psychological reasons that we'll cover later, we have selfish impulses all of the time, and we often aren't even aware of them. We do things without thinking of others; we put our needs above those of everyone else.

We've all heard about the importance of Looking Out for Number One, and there could be some truth to that maxim. But no one is an island, and we all rely on one another. And when it comes to relationships, we need to be able to take into account the hopes, feelings, aspirations and dreams of our partners. Selfishness isn't always a bad thing, but if it becomes the characteristic feature of how we relate to other people, our relationships will fail, and we will never find the deep fulfillment that a mutually-supportive, unconditionally loving relationship can bring.

Unconditional Love

Unconditional love is the opposite of self-absorption. Unconditional love is the ideal we must reach for if we want to realize the potential of our relationships and find true romantic fulfillment. It is a nearly divine principle which we should strive to incorporate not only into our love lives and romantic relationships, but also into our lives generally as much as possible.

To love unconditionally doesn't just mean to forgive the mistakes of your partner or of others. To love your partner unconditionally is to love them *for them*, because of *who they are*, not what they do. That means loving without expecting anything in return. They say that it is better to give than to receive. That may or may not be true; depending on the person — it *is* quite nice to receive. What's important though is the ability to give without the need, expectation or even the desire to get anything back in return.

This is true for giving gifts, for sex, and especially for love. Loving unconditionally is hard. Everybody wants to feel like their love is returned of course, but wanting and expecting to see a return for each of your gifts, or for your lover to reciprocate in everything you do, can be a trap. It's an ego trap because before long you slip into *needing* something back. And this can lead to Dependency, Demandingness, and Despondency (when you feel your love isn't being returned). Each of these three Ds is a relationship killer, and each is rooted in selfishness.

Self-Care and Compromise

Of course, every person needs to have their own

projects, their own goals, hopes and dreams. We all want these things to correspond with those of our romantic partners but we all have our own path to walk. I cannot walk on your path, and you cannot walk on mine. What we need is to be able to walk our paths together, to go forward together in the same direction, but in our own ways.

If you aren't attuned to the needs and goals of your partner, your relationship will never succeed. Relationships are all about support, and you can't support someone if you aren't interested in and engaged with their aspirations and life projects. This is obvious.

But it is also true that you cannot become *dependent* upon your partner. Dependency isn't just about money or resources. There are all sorts of successful, fulfilling relationships in which only one partner has access to money or other connections, though this sort of relationship can lead to problems. Dependency is mental. You are dependent on your partner when you become *too* fixated on their projects and their concerns without developing your own personal path.

While at first it might not seem to be so, dependency is just as much a problem of ego and selfishness as pure self-absorption and disregard for your partner's interest. Really, they are foils of one another. While the purely self-absorbed person selfishly disregards their partner's aspirations and feelings in favor of their own, the dependent person disregards *their own* aspirations in order to cling onto those of their partner. This is just as selfish, for the dependent person is relying entirely on their partner, without providing anything themselves. This isn't good for anyone.

The key is to be your own person, with your own goals, projects and dreams, but at the same time to be engaged with and attuned to the goals and dreams of your partner. This way, you and your partner(s) can grow and develop together, as equals sharing in the journey of life together. This means making room for and taking care of yourself, while always being ready to make compromises to accommodate your partner.

In this book, we'll explore the techniques for how you can do this, and incorporate unconditional, mutually affirming love into your life. But first, let's take a minute to talk about how and why we are selfish. The better we understand this common human trait, the better we will be able to improve ourselves and our relationships.

Chapter 2: The Origins of Selfishness

We're all taught from a very young age not to be selfish. We're told to share what we have with others, to respect other people, and to say "please" and "thank you." Children who fail to do any of these things will regularly be told by the nearest adult "not to be so selfish!" And yet, despite all of us going through this early conditioning, pretty much everyone is selfish at least some of the time. Why is that?

For centuries, there have been thinkers who were convinced that human beings are simply, at root, selfish beings. Perhaps the most famous of such thinkers is Thomas Hobbes, who argued that without the intervention of powerful autocratic governments, human beings necessarily exist in a constant state of war of all against all, where only the strongest or the cleverest would survive. Society, Hobbes argued, had to be compelled by force.

While not many people these days take Hobbes' theory very seriously as a story about the development of human society, the notion that people are at base selfish is still very common. Many people will blame all kinds of social problems on the basic fact that people are selfish and greedy. But is that true?

When you stop to think about yourself and your friends and loved ones, chances are that the primary characteristics you think of aren't greed and selfishness. Sure, you might recall how one time your brother wouldn't share his birthday cake, but overall we generally consider the people we know to be more or less kind and friendly people. It's hard to maintain any sort of relationship with someone who is wholly or even largely selfish.

So what gives? Clearly, we aren't all completely self-absorbed. But we also clearly aren't all completely selfless. The reality is that we are a mix, and there are all kinds of reasons for this. Let's look at them briefly.

Our Selfish Genes

In 1859, a book was written that would radically change scientific thinking forever. This book was, of course, Charles Darwin's *On the Origin of Species*. In it, Darwin first promoted the now universally familiar concept of natural selection, and what is now generally referred to as evolution.

The remarkable insight of Darwin and his colleagues into the gradual evolution of species over time has had a tremendous impact not just on our theories of biology and zoology, but on nearly every aspect of human and animal life. Certain thinkers, like Thomas Huxley (grandfather of the famous author Aldous Huxley) would see in Darwin's theory the confirmation of the Hobbesian idea of nature being inherently competitive and ego-centered.

However, not everyone agreed. Others, like Russian social thinker Peter Kropotkin, pointed out that while competition and individualism are certainly observable in nature, it's equally if not more common to find cooperation and mutual aid. When it comes to the survival of species, as in relationships, you need both.

Of course, this is not a book about evolution. But thinking about our evolutionary origin, we can see why selfish behaviors might permeate our lives, and we can better understand how to avoid them, to open ourselves up more to unconditional love and mutual support.

Humans are a social species, highly adept at cooperation. We have highly developed brains, and sophisticated linguistic abilities which allow us to communicate complex thoughts to each other, allowing us to work together on projects much too complicated for most other creatures. But while all that is true, from the perspective of our genetics, we are truly individualistic.

The concept of the Selfish Genes was popularized

by the British biologist Richard Dawkins in his 1976 book, *The Selfish Gene*. Dawkins furthers the Darwinian theory of evolution, armed with the new science of genetics, to argue that, as far as evolution is concerned, the most important thing is the transmission of our own genes. According to Dawkins, it isn't the species which drives evolution, but the genes. Because my genes are different from yours, I have an evolutionary reason to prefer my own satisfaction and success to yours. From the perspective of my genes, it is more important that I produce viable offspring than that you do.

We are, after all, organisms. And like any other organism, our primary biological function is to stay alive and to reproduce.

That said, we don't *just* want to survive. We want

to *thrive*. And thriving means all sorts of things, like comfort, love, friendship, and fun. And none of these things can be achieved just by ourselves. For probably all of human history, we've depended upon the company of other people. We've developed beyond a mere biological impulse to pass on our genes, but we can never leave that lineage behind completely.

Psychological Selfishness and Developing Empathy

The field of psychology grew by leaps and bounds in the 20th century, and we've learned a lot about the development of the human mind not just throughout our evolutionary history, but over the course of our individual lifetimes. The field of developmental psychology investigates not just the intricate structure of human decision making processes, but specifically looks at how those structures grow and change over time. The minds of children, researchers like the Swiss scientist Jean Piaget (1896-1980) and Russian researcher Lev Vygotsky (1896-1934) demonstrated, are very different than those of adults.

One thing we've learned about children is that they aren't born with a sense of the difference between themselves and others. Infants and very young people are literally unable to understand that their desires, preferences and attitudes are separate from the world around them. Before children learn to distinguish the fact that other people also have separate, equivalent, and private inner emotional lives, they must learn to distinguish the difference between themselves and others generally. And while kids pick it up pretty fast, it is something they learn.

Inspired by the work of Piaget in particular, Lawrence Kohlberg (1927-1987) developed a theory of moral development. Much like how Piaget described the development of children's cognitive skills as progressing through a series of stages, Kohlberg suggested that there are six distinct stages of moral development. These stages are sequential, and each stage represents a better approach to solving moral questions than the stage before it.

The brilliance of Kohlberg's work is to suggest a way to evaluate not just how strong or intelligent someone is, but that there can be variance in the degree to which a person can think ethically. And, crucially, that this is a capacity that is *developed*; not necessarily one which we are born with. Just like how most babies aren't able to appreciate good music, they aren't able to make moral decisions.

Some babies grow up to become great composers or musicians, or they may become expert musical listeners but some people don't. This is also true of our ability to make moral choices; some people get more advanced than others which means we should all practice!

The idea behind Kohlberg's theory is not to say that some people are more ethical than others, but people use different types of reasoning. The kinds of reasoning that people tend to use in the bottom stages, called the Pre-Conventional Stages, are the most selfish. In these stages, which are most common amongst children but are also expressed by adults, people act only according to what is directly good for them. They don't consider social values or laws, and they don't make decisions based on any sort of ethical principles.

An example of this sort of reasoning would be a child who steals a cookie just because he/she wants it, without thinking about the rules or the feelings of others. It is the logic of obedience and self-interest, of wanting to avoid punishment and wanting to get some sort of direct reward. A child who hasn't yet learned or accepted the rules of society is still in the first two stages. It's not until we know the difference between right and wrong, as the courts say, that we get to the next stages.

The middle two stages, called the Conventional

Stages, are maybe the most common form of moral reasoning we see. In the Conventional Stages of reasoning, people make decisions based on their understanding of social convention or laws and legal authority. This is certainly an improvement over the entirely egotistical, self-centered reasoning of the Pre-Conventional Stages, but notice how it isn't self*less*. The Conventional moral reasoner is still taking only *their* community's laws and *their* society's values into account. We often see politicians invoke this sort of reasoning, when they condemn behavior because it is illegal without actually addressing whether or not that behavior *should* be illegal.

It isn't until we get to the final stages that we see people making judgments based on ethical *principles*, independent of societal values, laws, or egotism. The final two stages are called the Post-Conventional Stages, also called the Principled Stages. The highest of the six stages is the stage of Universal Ethical Principles. This is, according to the moral development theory, the highest form of ethical reasoning that we humans can attain. And, when it comes to realizing the full potential of our relationships, this is the stage which we must strive to achieve.

We talked earlier about the importance of unconditional love in maintaining healthy, mutually-supportive relationships. Unconditional love is not something which comes easily to most people; in fact, it's something that is very hard to obtain even sporadically. It's a lofty moral goal; a universal ethical principle that belongs to the highest stage of moral development. That means that it's something we need to work hard to realize, and we need to be kind enough to ourselves to understand that we will sometimes fail. But it is in the trying that we become better persons, better partners, and will realize better relationships.

The principle of unconditional love is as far away from egotistical, low-level moral thinking as you can get. You don't offer your love because you want to avoid punishment (stage 1), or because you want to obtain some sort of direct personal benefit, like getting love back in return (stage 2). And of course, you don't offer love because it's popular amongst your friends to do so (stage 3) or because the law says so (stage 4). It's not even out of a regard for the general welfare of all (stage 5). In order to offer unconditional love, you have to believe in and strive after the universal principle, for its own sake.

The concept of moral development is a complicated one. People aren't always in one stage or another. Their moral judgments can vary from one stage to another, from one decision to the next, and sometimes people regress as well as progress through the stages. But what's important is that we can *all* do better. The more conscious we become of the underlying psychological basis for our actions and our decisions, the better we can understand our own hidden motivations. Only then do we have the tools to improve ourselves to become better partners, lovers, and human beings.

Sociology and Peer Pressure

There is one other big force on our developing self-absorbed and selfish attitudes and behaviors, and that's the social pressures we are faced with every day. It's no secret that we live in a highly competitive culture which has embraced the logic of competitive markets. Interestingly, the modern notions of economics being based on competition were developed around the same time as the idea that competition is characteristic of evolution. While the truth of both these attitudes can be questioned, there's no doubt that we live in a competitive, individualist culture.

Of course, that doesn't mean our culture is *wholly* individualistic. We celebrate those who make sacrifices to help others, we encourage

34

children to share and be kind, and we believe in the power of charities, governments and non-governmental organizations to help others.

All this is true, and yet we are constantly bombarded with messaging about the cutthroat nature of business or academia. Children are encouraged to compete for the highest grades so they can get in to the best school and land the best jobs. The national interest is conceived as being in competition with those of other nations. It's a dog-eat-dog world, they say, and in some ways that's true. In many of the largest and most profitable corporations, the emphasis on competition has grown so severe and people suffer such psychological stress that they feel unable to properly cooperate with their co-workers.

Even the political system is framed entirely in terms of a competition, in which the winner takes all, and it's sour grapes for the loser. All these assumptions about the organizational principle of competition go largely unchallenged and unrecognized. And these assumptions can invade and poison our relationships. When we internalize the dynamics of competition and individualism, it becomes difficult to open up fully and honestly with our partners. When we've been conditioned to see competition everywhere, it's hard not to import those attitudes into our love lives, which should be all about support and affection.

Perhaps the most damaging and obvious consequences of this problem is in the game-like attitude so many men take to dating, relationships and, primarily, sex. Viewing sexual encounters as scores on a tally that can be measured and compared against those of rivals and friends generates an atmosphere in which what should be intimate and personal encounters are objectified, devalued, and dehumanized. Sexual partners become not partners in adventure and play, but targets and notches on a belt. This attitude is commonly reflected in movies and media, and has become so widespread, particularly from the male perspective, that it affects pretty much every young person's development, and colors many of our relationships.

Because these sorts of attitudes are implicit and rarely spoken of directly, many people do not even recognize the extent to which these particular cultural values have impacted their own views about relationships. That can make them very hard to overcome when one is new to relationships, but these attitudes can also persist for a lifetime.

This is why it is so important to move beyond the Conventional Stages of moral reasoning, to embrace the higher levels of universal principles like unconditional love. Many of us may have seen problematic, egocentric relationship dynamics between our parents or other people in our community. The natural impulse is to emulate these behaviors, and we can do so without even realizing that that's what we are doing. Which is why it is so important to recognize the principle of unconditional love, so that we can invoke that standard to evaluate our own behavior, so that we can tell for ourselves whether we are setting ourselves up to realize the fullest potential of our relationships, or whether we are setting ourselves up to fall into the trap of selfishness and self-absorption.

We will always carry selfish impulses. That's okay, because they help us to survive and to drive us to succeed. But we all want to do more than just survive, we want to thrive. As social beings, the support, affection and love we receive in intimate relationships are some of the most valuable tools for thriving and living our most rewarding lives. If our selfish impulses get out of control, they can interfere with our ability to obtain those other things which are so important for us to thrive.

One of the most important and fulfilling parts of

life for many people is love and relationships, and relationships are by definition about concern not just for oneself, but for others. So now that we have a basis for understanding of some of the underlying causes of selfish behavior, we can start looking at what the benefits are of unselfish love and how to realize long, happy relationships.

Chapter: 3. Unselfish Love

We all carry within us the capacity for selfishness and for selflessness. No one will ever be fully one or fully the other. What we want to do, in order to realize the best relationships we can, is to limit our selfish impulses as much as possible, and foster unselfish love in our relations with others.

When we do this, we not only help ensure that we will hold onto the ones we love and enjoy the most in our relationships, but we also unlock the potential of having truly fulfilling and deep partnerships that only unconditional love makes possible. You can never experience the depth of pure love when you are harboring self-centered, egotistical motives and aspirations in your relationships. But when you let go of that baggage, you enter into the realm of love as a real partnership, and that is a well from which only good things flow.

Love as a Partnership

When we hear the word "partnership," we tend to think of businesses contacts and economic arrangements. But this word has much deeper, more profound meanings as well. A partner is someone with whom one has agreed to share in a project or endeavor. Partners are in it together, and the good of one is the good of all. In true partnerships, people can achieve together what they could never achieve alone. The union of distinct individuals into the act of a genuine partnership opens the way for greater success, satisfaction, and happiness.

Of course, this is true in any ideal partnership, but it is especially true of relationships. Two business partners who are ready at any minute to betray the other, and who keep secrets and manipulate the other, will never be as successful as a team of two honest, open and committed partners who share in the same goals and genuinely care for the wellbeing of the other. When you genuinely care for the other and you know that they genuinely care for you, then you don't have to stress or worry about betrayal or not getting your fair share.

Relationships as partnerships mean equality in love. That doesn't necessarily mean that there are no gendered divisions of labor or that each person must reciprocate every gesture with an equivalent one in return. That would be the very opposite of unconditional love. Equality in love means that each partner has the opportunity and support to follow their own ambitions and desires. It means the freedom for each to grow and become the person they hope to be. A healthy relationship is one which enhances each partner's ability to develop into the best person they can be. No one should be expected or forced to relinquish any part of their individuality for the sake of a relationship, and no relationship which demands that of anyone will ever be successful.

In relationships, this means you can let go of jealousy, which is a fear of betrayal and a feeling of possessiveness over your lovers. Jealousy is at root a self-centered, egotistical attitude. The jealous mind says *"this is mine, and what is mine belongs to no other."* Jealously is one of the most common and devastating relationship problems that can lead to heartbreak and even violence. Overcoming jealousy is one of the greatest benefits of unselfish love.

When you love unselfishly and unconditionally, there is no room for jealousy. Loving unconditionally means not expecting anything in return, and that means loving without an expectation of lifelong fidelity. It means loving without possessiveness, for you can never own a partner. A partner is an equal, a person with whom you are consensually engaged in the project of life. Accepting that not all things last forever, and that all things might change, allows you to let go of the base feelings of jealousy, possessiveness and mistrust which cause so many problems in relationships.

That doesn't mean that you have to accept that your partners will be running around promiscuously hooking up with everyone in town. Far from it. By allowing you to let go of jealousy and possessiveness, unselfish love allows you to develop the deep levels of trust in your partner so that you don't worry about whether they will betray you. You can only reach that level of trust in relationships when love is treated as a partnership, and we let go of our insecurities and baggage.

Unselfish love also means that people can accept their partners for who they are. Some people might not ever be able or willing to live monogamously, with only one romantic or sexual partner. Others embrace monogamy. It is important to have enough self-love and love for each other to be honest with your partner about your expectations and attitudes, because nothing is worse for a relationship than betrayal. If you are in a relationship with someone who cannot be faithful, but you genuinely need a faithful partner, then the best thing is to honestly and lovingly part ways. Other times, you may have a partner who cherishes the freedom of seeing other people. This isn't a betrayal if it is openly talked about and recognized by both partners, unselfishly and without jealousy. For some people, these sorts of relationships are wonderful. For others, they are not acceptable. It's important to know where your partner stands, and what their needs are.

Being attuned to the needs of your partner is what partnership is all about. As partners, what's good for one is good for both. If everyone involved in a relationship isn't able to pursue their own desires and follow what is good for themselves, then the relationship can never be a true partnership and will never be all that a relationship can be. Part of self-love and selfless love is honesty, both about what you need and want, and in recognition of what your lover needs and wants.

Self-love is not necessarily selfish love. The most healthy, vibrant relationships need just as much self-love as they do mutual-love. The key is to understand the difference between self-love and self-absorption.

Self-Love as Unselfish Love

To love yourself is to recognize your own authentic being, and to embrace and respect your true inner self. Notice how this is to move beyond the Conventional Stages of moral development mentioned earlier. Self-love is about seeking your own satisfaction not in the conventions, standards or values of the society around you. Self-love is about recognizing and nurturing your own authentic needs and desires. To recognize your authentic self, as opposed to the socially-constructed, inauthentic self, it is necessary to move away from the sorts of social insecurities that lead to predatory relationships, dependency, and jealousy.

It is only with a sufficient degree of self-love that we are able to fully and selflessly love another.

Unconditional love requires a level of emotional maturity and self-assuredness that can only come when you nurture and honor your authentic inner self. This means recognizing what you want and what you need from your relationships.

Once you're comfortable, open, and caring for yourself and your own needs, you can be genuinely caring and loving towards another. A partnership in which one member is reliant upon or dismissive of the other is no partnership at all.

While it may seem that someone who cares only about their own satisfaction and obtaining whatever rewards they can for themselves is engaging in self-love, the truth is that such a person is only hurting themselves through ignorance. This isn't true self-love, but self-absorption. The self-absorbed individual is blocking themselves off from the potential of deeply involved and intimate relationships with others, and is therefore doing themselves a great disservice. It's an old adage that the energy you put out is the energy you get back, and this is a prime example of that principle. A person who is self-absorbed will make themselves closed off to other people, and will necessarily be diminishing their own social potential, not just for romantic relationships but also for meaningful and stimulating friendships.

It may not be impossible for the self-absorbed person to live a happy live. But such a person will never be able to live life to the fullest extent possible. This is why self-love is not selfish love. Just as we all have selfish and competitive impulses, so too do we have social and cooperative impulses. This is part of our dual nature. The selfish or self-absorbed person blocks their cooperative nature, which is the higher expression of our social potential. The individual who practices self-love, however, is better able to balance their individuality and egoism with their social and compassionate sides. Thus the person who practices self-love is more complete, and is in a better position to obtain real genuine satisfaction from life.

Self-love allows one to develop their own authentic self. And when you're living authentically, you're much more likely to find the person who is right for you. Others will see that you are living as your true authentic self, and will be attracted to you for that reason. If you're already in a relationship, developing your authentic self will help you to maintain that relationship. You will inspire confidence in yourself as well as in others. And that's an important part of being in a relationship, helping to build up not just your own confidence, but the confidence of your partner.

Giving and Receiving Support

Mutual support is what relationships are all about. It's the ability of those in relationships to offer and receive support from one another that allows for the romantic partnership to propel the individuals further than they would have been able to go independently. Giving is just as important as receiving, as the stronger your partner is, the more support they will be able to offer you.

In order to best be supportive in a relationship, one necessarily has to escape from selfish and self-absorbed thinking. Being supportive means non-judgmentally, unconditionally standing behind your partner in all of his/her endeavors. This is not to say that disagreements never come up or shouldn't come up in healthy relationships. Rather, the point of being supportive is that you don't allow any differences of opinion or doubts to get in the way of your being in your partner's corner. In life, we are always presented with criticisms and challenges as we try to pursue our goals and projects, and it's important that in our relationships we have someone who will always be propping us up and encouraging us. We all have enough people in our lives to bring us down. In a relationship, it is your job to bring each other up.

This doesn't mean that there is no room to criticize your partner. Of course, dialogue and communication is one of the primary cornerstones of any healthy relationship. Rather, what it means is that any criticism must be done lovingly, from a genuine concern for the well-being of the other, and without any of your own ego entering into the equation. If your partner is suffering from some sort of addiction or other self-destructive pattern of behavior, you of course have a right and even an obligation to communicate your worries to them. But this must be done with the explicit intent of raising your partner up, not bringing him/her down.

In toxic relationships, it's not uncommon for an abusive partner to maintain power by constantly humiliating, criticizing and bringing down his/her more submissive partner. This is a terrible form of psychological manipulation that cannot be tolerated under any circumstances.

Being supportive does not mean fawning or being obsequious. It means caring enough about your partner to stand behind him/her no matter what. It means having the strength to swallow your pride when trivial disagreements arise, and to have the emotional maturity to address serious disagreements from a position of mutual support and unconditional love.

We've all seen couples who allow completely meaningless and trivial confrontations boil over and explode into full-blown shouting matches and arguments. This is an ego trap. When living closely with another person for any length of time, small annoyances are bound to pop up. This is unavoidable. The problem arises when people allow these trivial micro-confrontations to bottle up inside them and accumulate. Over time, unnecessary resentments develop. Eventually, the slightest, most irrelevant issue can trigger an overflow of pent-up emotions and suddenly you've got a vicious argument on your hand.

All of this could have been avoided if people had the emotional maturity to engage openly and honestly with each other in an environment of mutual support. Even the most saintly and goodly of persons will have some sort of annoying character trait or behavior that will get on somebody's nerves sooner or later. But if these things can be addressed openly without an atmosphere of hostility, then they become tiny matters to laugh about, instead of disastrous arguments which leave somebody sleeping on the couch (or worse).

An atmosphere of hostility is generated by the out-of-control ego, the selfish ego. It is the selfish ego which responds with hostility to criticisms or disagreements. In a supportive environment, one must be willing to accept criticism without identifying overly with the behavior criticized, and to offer criticism without judging the person for the behavior being criticized. To identify ourselves with our actions or to identify others with their actions is an ego-centered act. We must always try to remember that everyone is living their first life, and be forgiving and compassionate not just to our partners but to everyone.

If your lover expresses annoyance with you for having not made the bed properly, or for snoring too loudly, or for any other of life's infinite inconsequential transgressions, accept what they are saying without letting your ego leap up in defense of itself. At the end of the day, these things don't matter. So what if you don't care about making the bed, or if you don't think the turkey baster belongs in that drawer. It should always be more important that your partner *feels* upset or ticked off. You should care more about their emotional well-being than about being attached to your own trivial patterns of behavior.

At the same time, we should be confident enough in our supportive environments to feel comfortable expressing ourselves when something about our partner's behavior is grating upon us. It doesn't make you a bad person or a bad partner to feel annoyed by things which don't necessarily matter that much. We are all, after all, human, and humans have highly complex, inexplicable psychologies. Some people are neat freaks and need everything to be super tidy. Others couldn't care less about tidiness and much prefer the freedom to toss things where they may. The importance is in being open to communicate and compromise, and if your behavior is causing some sort of distress, and is easy to change, then your love for your partner should override any trivial preference.

However, unconditional love and support also means that when there are aspects of your partner's personality that he/she is unable or unwilling to change, that you still love and support him/her, non-judgmentally. Because really, how many of the things that most couples spend all day arguing about really matter? Almost all nasty arguments can be traced back to selfishness and the out of control ego. Sometimes there may be very deep-rooted differences in personalities that cannot be reconciled. Not all relationships are meant to last. But many people who care deeply for one another can get caught up in meaningless squabbles, and great potential can be lost because of lack of mutual support.

Succeeding Together

We mentioned earlier the importance of recognizing that no two people can ever walk the same path in life, and how a relationship is about walking down paths that go together in the same direction. That means that in a romantic partnership, each needs to feel free to pursue their own dreams and be their own person; to be encouraged to succeed and to be supported, even when what they are doing is very different from what their partner does.

Sure, maybe some sorts of people just shouldn't be together. A prison warden and an anti-incarceration activist probably won't ever be able to develop a mutually supportive and loving relationship. Their paths are simply trying to take them in opposite directions. But for most people, differences won't be so wide, and we need to be willing and able to accept that even in the most loving relationship, there will always be differences.

Even deep ethical differences can survive together in open and unconditionally loving relationships. For example, a vegetarian and a meat eater can, with mutual respect and sufficient self-love, live a happy life together, respecting and supporting the decisions of their partner while maintaining their own disagreement with their position.

When you love unselfishly, you leave it open for each person in a relationship to succeed in their own individual projects and aspirations. Because unconditionally loving relationships are mutually supportive, even if each partner has very different dreams, those dreams will be easier to realize because of the relationship. Selfish love leads to jealousy, possessiveness, and restrictions which hold back at least one member of the relationship from attaining their potential. When you love selflessly, everyone is furthered.

Some people are career-oriented and ambitious, and some people are not. It is not important that each member of a relationship be equally ambitious, or that each contribute equally to the finances of the partnership. For some people, this might be important, but it needn't be for everyone.

It is important to know that for authentic people, operating at a high level of moral reasoning necessary for selfless love, traditional gender roles need not apply. Some men are not career-oriented or driven to succeed in traditional competitive market settings, and some women are. Trying to force your partner to fit an inauthentic mold which doesn't suit them will never be successful. You cannot and should never expect to change people; you can only help elevate them, or hinder them and keep them down.

Of course, financial imbalances are a regular source of stress and conflict in relationships. Financial dependence can be as dangerous to a relationship as emotional dependence, and it is important that if one partner is reliant on the other financially, that this be an openly understood and agreed upon situation. It can be a great burden both financially and psychologically to have someone relying on you financially when you weren't planning for it.

That said, if you are looking for a partner who is rich and has lots of money, then you are not loving selflessly and unconditionally. You are looking out for yourself, and an authentic and mutually supportive relationship is not likely ever to materialize. People experienced in love, who have lived long and full lives, know that money doesn't matter. But a certain degree of independence and individualism is important, and staves off dependency. Part of self-love is taking responsibility for yourself, and contributing to your own upkeep as you contribute to the well-being of others.

Sometimes succeeding together means taking a back seat to allow your partner to prioritize their goals or ambitions. In life, we all go through ebbs and flows, and from one period to the next we can be much more or less busy. In the early stages of a relationship, it can be difficult to connect and grow together if one person is very busy and isn't able to make time for the relationship to be a priority. This is why for so many professionals it can be really hard to find romance. Unfortunately, in our current economic system and culture, people tend to have to work very long hours. This can put a lot of stress on relationships, particularly in the early stages.

Even when a relationship has developed, though, it can be quite difficult if one person is very busy and finds it difficult to prioritize the relationship. While being overly-career focused and ambitious can cause people to neglect their romantic partnerships in a selfish way, it's also true that sometimes, for periods at least, projects can come up that demand fuller attention. So long as this is not a permanent state of affairs, but a temporary situation to be gotten through, there is no reason why a healthy relationship cannot survive happy and intact. Developing the mindset of unselfish and unconditional love will help partners get through these periods.

By considering yourselves a partnership, the achievements of those with whom you are in a relationship are also your own achievements. You are always there in their corner, cheering them on and supporting them, as a key member of their team, even if you aren't on the payroll. Adopting this attitude can help couples get through trying times. And when you're very busy, there's nothing as refreshing and rejuvenating as having a dedicated, unselfish lover supporting you from the sidelines. It's this sort of mutual support that can propel people further in a relationship than they can get on their own.

Things don't always have to be reciprocal. If you only support your partner because you expect support back in return, then you aren't really loving unselfishly at all. You have to be willing to offer support and love as if you never expect your energies to be reciprocated. Of course, if you're in a mutually supportive and healthy relationship, those efforts will *certainly* be rewarded, but only if both partners have adopted the principle of unconditional love.

This might seem sort of like a paradox; you must not expect anything in return if you want to get the best returns. And maybe it is a bit of a paradox, but it is a moral lesson that is found again and again in all sorts of religions and philosophies, and we always seem to come back to it. Doing what's right is its own reward, but it also just happens to be true that if you do what is right and are a good person, certain benefits tend to accrue. Whether psychological or material or perhaps even spiritual, this pattern seems to repeat itself.

In relationships, it means that you will be at your strongest and best when you are offering unconditional love and support. For only then can you receive the same in return. And when a relationship has created an atmosphere of such unselfish and unconditional love, not only will it have become strong, healthy and very difficult to break, but also the support and rejuvenation made available to you by that strong healthy relationship will help you in all other aspects of your life. Tragedies become easier to deal with, fears and anxieties can more easily be dismissed, and the trials and tribulations of everyday life will lose some of their edge. Life will always provide challenges, but when you have a loving partner and a genuinely strong relationship, you have one of the strongest allies you can find in life.

Chapter 4: How to Overcome Selfishness

Now that we've discussed some of the root causes of selfishness, as well as some of the infinite benefits that come from developing a less selfish approach to relationships, you might be wondering how exactly to go about becoming less selfish. Everyone is told from the time they are very young that they shouldn't be selfish, and yet we are all selfish a lot of the time.

Being told and knowing that self-absorption is a negative personality trait, sadly, just isn't enough to actually change people's attitudes and behavior. The reason for this is simply that our behavior is *patterned*. While we were always being told as children not to be so selfish, we were also acting on natural biological impulses, as well as social pressures, to behave in selfish ways. Consequently, we all develop selfish psychological patterns that are deep rooted. Simply acknowledging that selfishness is a bad thing only touches the surface of our complicated minds. Deep down, at the root of selfishness, our unconscious minds need to break the patterns of selfishness.

Imagine the mind as an iceberg, floating in the ocean. We've all heard the expression "just the tip of the iceberg." Well, when it comes to our minds, the conscious, reasoning part is just the tip. Below the surface of our awareness is an immense cognitive structure which we are nearly always completely unaware of. This is called the unconscious mind, and it has occupied the thoughts of philosophers and psychologists for as long as those fields have existed.

Even Plato, over two thousand years ago, wondered about the unconscious mind. Of course, he didn't use the terms the way we do now, which come largely from the 19th and 20th century works of great psychologists like Sigmund Freud (1856-1939) and Carl Jung (1875-1961). Plato conceived of the human mind as comprising three parts, and he viewed it as being like a chariot, with two horses pulling a charioteer. The charioteer, what we might call the conscious mind, has some degree of control over the two horses, but it is always the horses that do the pulling. One horse, the appetitive, desirous horse, is bad spirited, while the other, the moral and passionate one, is of a good nature. Both horses are always somewhat in a state of conflict, and it is the challenge of the charioteer to steer them towards higher truths.

This is, of course, a complex metaphor, and Plato wasn't talking about relationships. But it shows how far back goes human thinking about how to harness the unconscious aspect of our mind. Carl Jung saw dreams as being a window into our unconscious mind, and surrealist artists like Max Ernst and Andre Breton attempted to harness them as inspiration for art.

Over the ages, many techniques have been developed and attempted to gain access to our unconscious mind, from meditation and art to psychotherapy and hallucinogenic drugs. In some meditative practices, the goal is the complete dissolution of the ego. This is the task of a lifetime (or who knows, maybe several!) and isn't the point of this book. We aren't looking to abolish the ego entirely, what we want to do is to keep it in check, and unlearn some of the selfish patterns our unconscious mind has developed.

We're going to talk about the things you can do in everyday life to help you overcome selfishness in your relationships. This will help you become a better partner and lover, and will help you to avoid some common relationship pitfalls. Hopefully, this will help you live a happier, fuller life.

Checking Yourself: The Importance of Self- Monitoring

The key to all self-improvement and especially the attempt to overcome selfishness is to get in the habit of monitoring your own thoughts and actions. This is called checking yourself, and it is an important practice that has all sorts of benefits even beyond the realm of happy, fulfilling relationships. You want to reach a stage where you are aware of what you are doing *and why* as much as possible. This may sound like the easiest thing in the world, but you might be surprised!

Take, for example, your breathing. Are you breathing through your mouth, or your nose? If through your nose, which nostril? Have you ever noticed that you almost always breathe through only one nostril, or the other? Now that you're thinking about your breathing, you can notice all sorts of things about it. But you've been breathing all day, and for your whole life! You're almost *never* aware of it, and it's happening all the time!

When it comes to monitoring your own thoughts and actions, things get even more complicated and subtle. And this is where the practice of checking yourself comes in. Say you find yourself annoyed with your partner for some reason. As soon as you realize you are annoyed, stop and think. *Why* are you annoyed? Is it something they said, or something they forgot to do? Ask yourself, what is it that upset you about what they did, or said?

Now, sometimes they might have done or said something that was hurtful or offensive, and if that is the case, then you might feel yourself get angry. Whenever you feel yourself get angry, try not to react. Anger is an egocentric response, and it often comes when we feel insulted, and we feel that we as a person have been attacked or if we feel that we are being ignored. But notice that these are all selfish attitudes. It's all about *us* with anger. Anger has no place in an unconditionally loving relationship. Of course, it is bound to pop up! But you just need to recognize it for what it is, and allow it to dissipate. Once it has dissipated, you can talk to your partner about what it is he/she has done that has made you angry, and explain to him/her how it made you feel. We'll talk more about communication in the next chapter.

So, that's anger. Notice that it is happening, allow it to subside, and when you are no longer angry, you can talk to your partner about how his/her behavior made you feel. But so many conflicts don't begin with anger. They begin with tiny little insignificant things, which accumulate and eventually boil over into a big enormous conflict. This can be avoided, if you develop the practice of checking yourself.

As soon as you feel annoyed about something —whether it's the bathroom not having been cleaned, or your partner showing up late for a movie — instead of allowing that minor negative emotion to accumulate within you, stop and check yourself. Ask yourself why it is that you feel annoyed. How important, really, is their being late, for example? People are late for things all the time. Until they get there, you'll have no way of knowing *why* they are late, so there is no use feeling annoyed. After all, being grumpy won't make them less late anyway.

More often than not, when you check yourself

you will find that the things that are making you upset are so meaningless and so trivial, that it's silly even to get hung up on them. The more often you get into the habit of checking yourself, the sooner you will come to see that it is your deeply rooted selfish mind —the ego —which is getting hung up on these minor things, and you will come to see how ridiculous the ego can sometimes be.

Very often, when there is a disagreement or an argument, one's impulse is to take offense. When you take offense, you tend to react, and in response the other person reacts, and now you've got an argument on your hands. The whole thing can be avoided if you don't *react*. You want to *act*, without *reacting*. If your partner criticizes you, try not to get offended, even if he/she said something offensive. Check yourself, and see that you want to react to the perceived insult, because your ego has been damaged. Try never to allow your ego to take control this way. Don't react, but act.

To act without reacting is to address the situation in the best way possible, rather than in the way it feels most immediately gratifying. Sometimes yelling at someone or getting into an argument *feels good* at the time, even though it leads to disaster and regret immediately afterwards. So don't react, but act. When an argument is beginning, act to stop it before it can get underway. One of the most useful techniques for diffusing an argument is to acknowledge how your partner feels, make him/her feel that you are listening to him/her. This doesn't mean that you have to agree with what he/she is saying. It doesn't mean that you have to accept it. But far more important than winning an argument is being supportive. That is the key to a strong relationship.

Your partner accuses you of never doing the dishes. Instead of responding immediately that you just did the dishes the day before or two days ago or whatever, check yourself. Notice that you are getting upset over nothing. There is no reason to have an argument over dishes! Tell your partner that you understand what he/she is saying. Acknowledge his/her feelings, and tell him/her that you didn't mean to upset him/her. Now you aren't in an argument anymore. You can ask him/her why he/she feels that you never do the dishes, if there are too many dishes piling up, or maybe he/she is actually upset about something else which he/she wasn't communicating about, and the dishes not being done was simply a trigger releasing those emotions. Because you *acted* without *reacting*, you can get to the heart of what the problem is. And maybe it turns out there really isn't a problem, or it turns out that the problem is something else. But the most important thing is that you didn't get into an emotionally traumatizing argument over something as trivial as a few dirty dishes.

When you check yourself, and you prevent yourself from getting worked up or from reacting without thinking, you intervene with your unconscious selfish patterns before they can be realized. Every time you intervene with a selfish pattern, that pattern gets weaker, and you build up a selfless compassionate pattern to take its place. Now if you are quite selfish, your selfish patterns will be much stronger than your compassionate, selfless ones to begin with. But if you keep remembering to check yourself as much as possible, day by day your selfish patterns will grow weaker and weaker, and it will become easier and easier to act unselfishly.

As it becomes more automatic and easier to act selflessly, you will find it much easier to embrace unconditional love for your partner. And once that begins happening, the relationship can become mutually supportive, and it will be strong and resilient and very difficult to break. Instead of getting into trivial arguments, you will help each other overcome barriers and obstacles, and support each other along the path of life.

Taking Up Space

Another important part of checking yourself deserves its own special mention. This is called taking up space. Whenever we are involved with other people, whether it is in a classroom, an office, a group of friends or in a relationship, we are always communicating with one another, and exchanging thoughts and ideas. Unless people are being completely silent, or everyone is all talking at once, there is usually only one speaker at a time. This is what it means to take up space; it's not about how much of a room your body fills, but how much you are dominating an interaction at a particular time and place.

Different people, with different minds and

psychologies, tend to take up more or less space.
Some people feel more comfortable in certain
contexts and situations, and so will take up more
space than they would in other contexts and
some people who might take up a lot of space
with people they know and are very comfortable
with, might step back a lot when with strangers
or unfamiliar people. This is all natural. It is
never the goal to take up as much or as little
space as possible. But what is important is
balance.

When it comes to taking up space, balance
means both being aware of how much space you
are taking up in a conversation relative to the
other participants, as well as considering what
your proper role in the situation is. A university
professor giving a lecture to two hundred

students will take up far more space than anyone else in the room, and that's okay. But if you take up that much space in your relationship, you have a serious problem.

People are all different, but generally speaking, women tend to take up less space than men in situations where both men and women are present. There are various complicated social and psychological reasons for this, but it isn't because women have less to say or because men are more interesting. This is where the concept of stepping up and stepping back comes from, and it is a very important concept not just in relationships, but in any sort of communication.

If, in checking and monitoring yourself, you find that you are taking up way more space than other people, then you should consider *stepping back*. That means see what happens if you open the floor up for other voices. You may find that people who have been silent will start speaking.

Conversely, if you tend to stay pretty quiet, you should consider *stepping up*. That means putting yourself out there, and having your voice heard. You may just find that people will really value what you have to say.

In a relationship, this is extremely important. If you monitor yourself and find that you are either making all of the decisions, or not making any of the decisions, then you should consider stepping up or stepping back. The purpose of monitoring how much space you take up isn't just to make sure you are taking up more space if you tend to be quiet or less space if you tend to take up more. The point is in finding the proper balance. And this balance is completely relative to the context. Maybe your partner is completely comfortable not making decisions, and is completely happy hanging back in that way. But it is still important to give them the opportunity to step up, otherwise neither of you might ever know.

On the other hand, if you find that you aren't taking up very much space, and that you tend to be more submissive in a relationship, you should consider stepping up, too. It doesn't mean that everyone must always take up an equal amount of space, but everyone should find where their comfort level is, and then push it a bit. If you are comfortable speaking a lot and have a response to everything, or always have an idea for date night and have all sorts of plans, try going outside of your comfort zone a little to let your partner make the plans for the evening, or let other people speak. If you're usually more than happy being led and don't usually make plans, put yourself out there a bit and take control for an evening.

By monitoring how much space we take up in relationships (and in life in general), we give our partners and ourselves the opportunity to get outside of our comfort zones, and develop as caring, communicative people. Providing an atmosphere that creates this sort of opportunity for mutual growth is what a genuinely loving relationship is all about.

Giving Without Receiving

Already mentioned several times in this book, one of the most absolutely important habits to develop to maintain a healthy, mutually supportive and lasting relationship is to practice giving without receiving. That means to give without expecting anything in return, genuinely unselfish acts. Not only will this make your partner feel loved and appreciated, it will help you to overcome your ego and your selfish impulses, and will make your relationship stronger.

To practice giving without receiving is easy. Simply do nice things for your partner, without the expectation that you will receive anything back. You might receive something back, or you might not. Derive joy merely from the act of doing something nice for your partner. You can make him/her breakfast or dinner without expecting any thanks or expecting him/her to make you dinner the next night. Maybe he/she will thank you; it doesn't matter. You do these things out of love for him/her and that alone; any additional benefits that might come your way are just a bonus.

Perhaps the most challenging domain for giving without receiving is the domain of sex. Culturally and socially, we are conditioned to think of sex as a sort of conquest, or a taking. This is, sadly, especially true of men. This thinking must be entirely abandoned.

In order to practice giving without expecting anything in return when it comes to sex and love, there's nothing especially complicated you have to do. It's actually very simple. But it's very much against our socially derived instincts!

Every now and then, consider pleasuring your partner without him/her returning the favor. You can give him/her oral sex or give him/her a sexual massage without any expectation or plan that when you are finished, he/she will turn around and do the same for you. Make sex an expression of love, a gift that you give to your partner, rather than a merely pleasant physical act.

The principle of unselfishly giving without receiving isn't about keeping accounts or refusing gifts in return, it is about adopting a certain mental attitude towards acts of affection or love. Doing nice things for your partner is its own reward, even if you get other rewards out of it. It's about developing a more loving, less selfish mind.

Chapter 5: The Benefits of Unselfish Love

Of course, we've been talking all along about the benefits that accrue from overcoming selfishness in relationships. The obvious and most important benefit is in creating healthier, more resilient and successful relationships, but there are other benefits as well. In this final chapter, let's go over what these rewards are for loving unselfishly.

The Expanded Perspective: Learning from Others' Point of View

As we've said, the entire purpose of a great relationship is to develop a partnership with another person. The partnership is stronger than the individuals alone, and the strength of such a partnership helps people get through difficult times, and to grow and develop more fully as people.

One of the greatest advantages to finding such a partner in life is the expanded perspective you get being so intimately involved with another. When you love unselfishly, you allow yourself more easily to gain access to your partner's perspective. The ego and the selfish mind will always want to reject any perspective that is not its own, but the more you learn to love unselfishly, the more you can learn from your partner.

A loving relationship can help you learn about who you are. A supportive partner can help reveal to you things about yourself that you might not have recognized. The support that comes from an environment of unconditional love can give you the confidence to pursue creative projects you might not otherwise have done.

Most importantly, a deep and intimate relationship helps us to get a glimpse of the world from someone else's perspective. Everyone comes from a different background, and has different experiences as they grow in the world. By sharing a life with someone unselfishly, you can gain some of the insights from their unique perspective. You can never, nor would you ever want, to get their complete perspective, for you are always the locus of your own experience. But you can learn about what the world is like from the standpoint of a different gender, or culture, or age, or whatever differences exist between you and your partner. No two people are alike. And this is the kind of knowledge that can help us not only in our romantic relationships, but also can help create stronger, more resilient communities.

Communication: The Root of Healthy Relationships

It's an age-old expression that communication is at the heart of any great relationship, and this is true. The biggest limitation to developing healthy communicative habits is the selfish impulses of the unconscious mind —the ego. The more you can overcome these as you grow in your relationships, the better your communication becomes, and the less liable you are to succumb to trivial and pointless arguments and disagreements.

When you monitor your own emotional state to avoid reacting in anger or out of fear and jealousy, you overcome a major source of stress and open yourself up to stimulating dialogues that otherwise would have been swept away in a useless torrent of angry words. When you are able to have a dialogue instead of an argument, you not only might save your relationship, but also both you and your partner are presented with an opportunity to grow as people that might otherwise have been completely missed.

The benefits of healthy communication that come from a mutually supportive and unselfishly loving relationship also extend out beyond your romantic life and improve your ability to communicate with people in all kinds of contexts. Learning how to monitor how much space you take up can lead to more productive and rewarding work environments, better relationships with your family and friends, and the opportunity to benefit from the opinions and perspectives of people you might not have listened to before.

Or, on the other hand, in learning to step up and move out of your comfort zone, you might find yourself with a new degree of control in your relationship which you've always wanted. And this too can spread to other areas of your life. Gaining the confidence to speak up amongst your friends or at work can be a great boost of confidence, and the world will benefit from hearing your voice.

Relationships often get hung up on really dumb and pointless arguments. We've all seen it. We've all done it. When you develop healthy communication, and learn that the first step to avoid a useless *confrontation* and to turn it into a productive *conversation* is to monitor your own emotions, try to check yourself before you react.

Life as Play

At the end of the day, we are all only alive for a short moment on Earth. During that time, we face all sorts of challenges and trials, but we also experience all the beauty and wonder that there is to find here in this world. One of the most wonderful and amazing things you can find in life is a loving partner.

Being in a healthy relationship is all about playing together. When you realize how trivial so many of the egocentric arguments you tend to have are, and how self-absorbed people can be, you get a better sense of what really does matter. What's really important is the joy of life, and the opportunity we have to share that joy with others.

When we live life as play, we live with compassion. We forgive the mistakes of others, and instead of getting angry, we laugh it off. We find joy in the little things, like preparing meals or watching a movie. These are all activities which gain a special significance in the context of an unselfish, mutually supportive, loving relationship. Accepting the principle of universal love over self-absorption isn't necessarily easy, and we'll never be fully successful but it's the goal to which we must strive if we want to realize the greatest potential in our relationships.

Other books and Audio by the author

Charisma: How to Captivate People

Narcissistic Personality Disorder: Narcissistic Men and Women How to Spot Them, Check Them and Then Avoid Them

The Killer Instinct: Creating the Mindset to Achieve Your Maximum Potential

Made in United States
North Haven, CT
24 December 2021

13544601R00059